GETTING TO KNOW THE WORLD'S GREATEST ARTISTS

HENRI
ROUSSEAU

WRITTEN AND ILLUSTRATED BY MIKE VENEZIA

CHILDREN'S PRESS®
A DIVISION OF SCHOLASTIC INC.
NEW YORK TORONTO LONDON AUCKLAND SYDNEY
MEXICO CITY NEW DELHI HONG KONG
DANBURY, CONNECTICUT

Cover: *Fight of a Tiger and Buffalo,* by Henri Rousseau. 1908, oil on canvas, 170 x 189.5 cm. © Cleveland Museum of Art, Gift of the Hanna Fund, 1949.186.

Colorist for illustrations: Dave Ludwig

Library of Congress Cataloging-in-Publication Data

Venezia, Mike.
    Henri Rousseau / written and illustrated by Mike Venezia.
        p. cm. — (Getting to know the world's greatest artists)
    Summary: An introduction to the life and work of the nineteenth-century French artist Henri Rousseau.
    ISBN 0-516-22495-6 (lib. bdg.)   0-516-26998-4 (pbk.)
        1. Rousseau, Henri Julien Félix, 1844-1910—Juvenile literature. 2. Painters—France—Biography—
Juvenile literature. 3. Primitivism in art—France—Juvenile literature. [1. Rousseau, Henri Julien Félix, 1844-
1910. 2. Artists.] I. Rousseau, Henri Julien Félix, 1844-1910. II. Title.

ND553.R67 V465 2002
759.4—dc21
[B]

2001047199

Henri Rousseau was born in Laval, France, in 1844. Even though he never had any art lessons, Henri believed with all his heart that if he worked hard enough, he would someday become a great artist.

The Waterfall, by Henri Rousseau. 1910,
oil on canvas, 116.2 x 150.2 cm.
© Art Institute of Chicago, Helen Birch
Bartlett Memorial Collection, 1926.262.

Henri Rousseau is best known for his jungle paintings. At first, these pictures might seem a little childlike. Jungle plants, leaves of trees, and flowers are way oversized. Sometimes, the people and animals seem stiff and flat.

Tropical Landscape-An American Indian Struggling with an Ape, by Henri Rousseau. 1910, oil on canvas, 113.6 x 162.5 cm. © Virginia Museum of Fine Arts, Richmond, Collection of Mr. and Mrs. Paul Mellon.

In some of Henri's jungle paintings, odd things are going on. In the painting above, an American Indian is fighting with a gorilla! In *The Merry Jesters*, monkeys in the middle of a deep, dark jungle are playing with a back scratcher and a milk bottle.

At first, people couldn't stand Rousseau's paintings. They thought he wasn't a serious artist and they wanted to know why he put all those strange things in his pictures.

On the Bank of the Seine, Bennecourt, by Claude Monet. 1868, oil on canvas, 81.5 x 100.7 cm. © Art Institute of Chicago, Potter Palmer Collection, 1922.427.

Two Sisters (On the Terrace), by Pierre Auguste Renoir. 1881, oil on canvas, 100.5 x 81 cm. © Art Institute of Chicago, Mr. and Mrs. Lewis Larned Coburn Memorial Collection, 1933.455.

At the end of the nineteenth century, people had just gotten used to the paintings of Claude Monet, Pierre August Renoir, and the rest of the Impressionist artists. They also were used to paintings done by earlier artists, such as Eugene Delacroix and Théodore Géricault.

Officer of the Imperial Guard on Horseback, by Théodore Géricault. 1812, oil on canvas, 349 x 266 cm. © Art Resource, NY/The Louvre, Paris, France, photo by Erich Lessing.

For years, people expected a good painting to look as realistic as possible. They wanted to see carefully painted figures as well as perspective, which gave everything a feeling of space and being real. It took many years before people appreciated Henri Rousseau's beautifully colored, imaginative, flatter-looking paintings.

Algerian Women in their Apartment, by Eugene Delacroix. 1834, oil on canvas, 180 x 229 cm. © Art Resource, NY/ Réunion des Musées Nationaux, photo by Arnaudet/J. Schormans.

Porte Beucheresse, à Laval,
by Jean-Baptiste Messager. 1872,
engraving, copper plate on paper.
© Musée du Vieux-Château, Laval,
photo by Monsieur Charbonnier.

Henri Rousseau lived in an amazing home when he was growing up in Laval. It was actually part of a gated tower that had been built hundreds of years earlier to protect his town. Henri Rousseau always had a great imagination. He must have had lots of fun playing with his friends when he was a kid.

11

Henri Rousseau's great imagination was one of the best things about him. Sometimes, though, he let his imagination run a little bit out of control.

Henri didn't do very well in school—except in art and music. He often blamed his parents for not recognizing his talent and sending him to art school. If they had, Henri later told people, he would have been the wealthiest and most famous artist in France. But even without his parents' help, Henri was determined to be an artist someday, no matter what.

Artillerymen (Les Artilleurs), by Henri Rousseau. c. 1894, oil on canvas, 79.1 x 98.9 cm. © Solomon R. Guggenheim Museum, New York, Gift of Solomon R. Guggenheim, 1938, #38.711, photo by David Heald.

Henri often made up stories about himself that weren't exactly true. He told people that when he was a young man in the French army, he fought in the jungles of Mexico. Everyone believed this was where Henri Rousseau got ideas for his jungle paintings.

The truth was that while Henri Rousseau's army group was off fighting in Mexico, Henri was spending a month in jail. Before he joined the army, Henri had become mixed up with some bad kids. They ended up stealing money and postage stamps from a lawyer's office where Henri had once worked.

After Henri Rousseau finished up his jail sentence and army duties, he was ready to begin his life. Henri met and fell in love with a girl named Clemence Boitard. In 1869, Henri and Clemence got married and moved to Paris, France. In Paris, Henri got a job in the French customs office.

The Toll House, by Henri Rousseau. c. 1890, oil on canvas, 40.6 x 32.8 cm. © Bridgeman Art Library International Ltd., London/New York/ Courtauld Gallery, London, UK.

Henri made sure taxes were paid on anything coming into the city. It was a pretty boring job, but Henri's bosses were nice enough to let him draw and practice his art. The painting above by Henri shows one of the customs stations where he worked.

The Bridge at Sevres, by Henri Rousseau. 1908, oil on canvas. © Art Resource, NY/Scala/
Pushkin Museum of Fine Arts, Moscow.

Henri Rousseau learned everything about art on his own. Sometimes he went to art museums and copied the works of great artists. He also copied figures and objects from postcards, books, and magazines. Henri loved to spend his Sundays painting scenes in different areas of Paris.

*View of Malakoff,
Hauts-de-Seine,*
by Henri Rousseau.
1908, oil on canvas.
© Bridgeman
Art Library
International Ltd.,
London/New York/
Private Collection.

One of his favorite places to paint was the Jardin des Plantes. This was a huge greenhouse filled with plants and trees from all over the world. When he entered the Jardin, Henri said, he felt as if he had entered a dream!

Photograph of the Jardin des Plantes.
© Corbis-Bettmann/Robert Holmes.

When Henri felt ready to show his artwork, he tried to get it into the Paris Salon. The Salon was the most important art show in the world. The Salon judges wouldn't even look at Henri's paintings, though.

Fortunately, there was another art show going on at the same time. It was called the Salon des Independents. This salon would let anyone show their artwork!

One of the first paintings Henri showed there was *Carnival Evening*. Most people said it looked naïve, which means childlike. But one famous Impressionist artist liked it a lot. Camille Pissarro thought Henri's painting was great. He especially liked the beautiful colors.

Carnival Evening, by Henri Rousseau. 1886, oil on canvas, 117.3 x 89.5 cm.
© Philadelphia Museum of Art, The Louis E. Stern Collection.

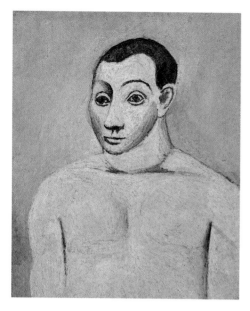

Self-Portrait, by Pablo Picasso. 1906, oil on canvas, 65 x 54 cm. © Art Resource, NY/Réunion des Musées Nationaux/Musee Picasso, Paris, France/ ARS, NY.

Portrait of Georges Seurat, by Ernest J. Laurent. 1883, charcoal on paper. © Art Resource, NY/Réunion des Musées Nationaux/ Louvre, Paris, France, photo by C. Jean.

Self-Portrait with Hat. In the background Manao Tupapau, by Paul Gauguin. c. 1893, oil on canvas, 46 x 38 cm. © Art Resource, NY/Musée d'Orsay, Paris, France, photo by Erich Lessing.

Other famous artists appreciated Henri Rousseau's work, too. Pablo Picasso, Georges Seurat, and Paul Gauguin were some of the artists who knew Henri Rousseau had a special and remarkable talent. Henri had many artist friends who encouraged him to keep painting and show everyone he really was a great artist.

Engraving of the 1889 World's Fair. © The Art Archive/Musée Carnavalet, Paris, France/Dagli Orti.

In 1889, something happened that changed Henri Rousseau's artwork forever. The World's Fair came to Paris. Henri was able to see how people from all over the world lived. He dreamed about mysterious, faraway lands and began showing these dreams in his paintings.

Tiger in a Tropical Storm (Surprised!), by Henri Rousseau. c. 1891, oil on canvas, 129.8 x 161.9 cm. © National Gallery, London.

Soon after the World's Fair ended, Henri Rousseau created his first jungle painting. It's called *Surprised!* and shows a fierce tiger caught in a rainstorm. The moody feeling of windblown trees surrounding a frightened tiger got the attention of more people than ever before. What everyone really liked, though, was Henri's use of color. There are so many different and beautiful shades of green in this painting it's hard to count them all.

War, or The Horseride of Discord, by Henri Rousseau. 1894, oil on canvas, 114 x 195 cm.
© Art Resource, NY/Réunion des Musées Nationaux/Musée d'Orsay, Paris, France.

Even though *Surprised!* was leading the way to Henri's dream of becoming a famous artist, he didn't paint another jungle picture for almost ten years. Instead, Henri created many other powerful and mysterious works.

The Sleeping Gypsy, by Henri Rousseau. 1897, oil on canvas, 129.5 x 200.7 cm.
© Museum of Modern Art, New York, Gift of Mrs. Simon Guggenheim.

In *War,* Henri showed a terrifying woman riding a frightening black horse to represent the horrors of war. *The Sleeping Gypsy* shows the strange meeting of a curious lion and a sleeping musician. This quiet moment on a moonlit night in the middle of the desert is one of Rousseau's most famous paintings.

The Football Players (Les Jouers de Football), by Henri Rousseau. 1908, oil on canvas, 100.5 x 80.3 cm. © Solomon R. Guggenheim Museum, New York.

In 1893, when Henri Rousseau was 49 years old, he decided to quit his job at the customs office and become a full-time artist. But he never had an easy time of it. Even though his paintings were slowly catching on, many people still made fun of them.

The Centennial of Independence, by Henri Rousseau. 1892, oil on canvas, 112 x 157 cm. © J. Paul Getty Museum, Los Angeles, CA, 88.PA.58.

Henri Rousseau refused to let these critics discourage him. He continued to create paintings that are considered today to be some of the most mysterious and beautiful works of art ever done.

Exotic Landscape, by Henri Rousseau. 1910, oil on canvas, 130 x 162 cm. © Bridgeman Art Library International Ltd., London/New York/Norton Simon Collection, Pasadena, CA, USA.

Virgin Forest with Setting Sun, or Black Man Attacked by Jaguar, by Henri Rousseau.
c. 1910, oil on canvas, 114 x 162 cm. © Art Resource, NY/Kunstmuseum, Basel,
Switzerland/Giraudon.

When Henri started painting his jungle
pictures again, he became so involved in them
that he sometimes frightened himself. While he
was working on *Virgin Forest with Setting Sun*,
Henri had to run and open a window to catch
his breath.

Henri Rousseau died in 1910 at the age of 66. The most important thing to Henri was not only to be a great artist, but to be known as a great artist as well. Near the end of his life, Henri Rousseau's dream finally came true.

Works of art in this book can be seen at the following places:
The Art Institute of Chicago, Chicago
Cleveland Museum of Art, Cleveland
Courtauld Gallery, London
J. Paul Getty Museum, Los Angeles
Kunstmuseum, Basel
The Louvre, Paris
Musée d'Orsay, Paris
Musée Picasso, Paris
Museum of Modern Art, New York
National Gallery of Art, Prague
Norton Simon Collection, Pasadena
Philadelphia Museum of Art, Philadelphia
Pushkin Museum of Fine Arts, Moscow
Solomon R. Guggenheim Museum, New York
Virginia Museum of Fine Arts, Richmond